Praise for *Black Mestiza*

"*Black Mestiza* is astonishing in its beauty, sincerity, sonorous power, and passion. The cry of loving, complicated women, the call of the sea, the spill of writerly ghosts, the clash of languages, the press and pull of Florida and the speaker's ancestors lift and embolden this collection. *Black Mestiza* is a searing, complex love letter and we're all so fortunate Aldana is writing poetry right now. A glorious collection."—Jennifer Maritza McCauley, author of *When Trying to Return Home* and *Kinds of Grace*

"Yael Valencia Aldana's *Black Mestiza* investigates a complex matriarchal genealogy as we learn in the first poem: 'Mother, no men stay in our family.' The sacred feminine of goddesses and the *abuela*, the Anglican prayer book and voodoo, Instagram and bodegas, Margaret Atwood and Angela Davis, Zora Neale Hurston and Sandra Cisneros, all swirl in these poems of wonder and reclamation. Through litany, abecedarian, haiku, cento, pantoum, and stereoscope, Aldana creates a world of connection, becoming her own materfamilias as she raises her son. She is an important voice to be reckoned with: 'Because you cannot hear me / doesn't mean I am not singing.'"—Denise Duhamel, author of *Second Story*

"'We are of the Caribbean / our names mean salt water in the veins . . .' This seems to be the book's intention: to reveal the sting and salve, like salt water, of the Caribbean mestiza identity and experience. The poems don't side with the sting or with the salve, which is a refreshing perspective for such a historically loaded and still deeply personal topic."—darlene anita scott, author of *Marrow: Poems*

T0286711

"The speaker in Yael Valencia Aldana's debut collection, *Black Mestiza*, declares early on, 'I know how to stand in more / than one place at a time.' These poems bear witness to her lyric standing, both firm and fluid, the speaker's many simultaneous identities kaleidoscopically explored. Herein, a missing grandmother is summoned, along with a birth mother, an adoptive mother, and the speaker as mother: 'ancestors come to the fore,' advisers across eras and oceans. *Black Mestiza* welcomes many voices, many twined histories, in this powerful reckoning."—Julie Marie Wade, author of *Quick Change Artist* and *Skirted*

BLACK MESTIZA

BLACK
MESTIZA

poems

YAEL VALENCIA ALDANA

 UNIVERSITY PRESS OF KENTUCKY

Gloria Anzaldúa's quote is from *Borderlands/La Frontera: The New Mestiza*. Copyright ©
1987. Reprinted by permission of Aunt Lute Books.
"Things To Do Today" from *It Is If I Speak*. © 2000 by Joe Wenderoth. Published by
Wesleyan University Press. Used by permission.
Lucille Clifton, excerpt from "the thirty-eighth year" from *How to Carry Water: Selected
Poems*. Copyright © 1974, 1987 by Lucille Clifton. Reprinted with the permission of The
Permissions Company, LLC on behalf of BOA Editions, Ltd., boaeditions.org
Ruth Behar quote from *Translated Woman: Crossing the Border with Esperanza's Story*
(Tenth Anniversary Edition, 2003) is used with permission from Beacon Press;
permission conveyed through Copyright Clearance Center, Inc.
A note to the reader: The poems in this volume employ racial slurs and other sensitive
language to describe historical and contemporary instances of racism and
oppression. Discretion is advised.

Scholarly publisher for the Commonwealth, serving Bellarmine University, Berea
College, Centre College of Kentucky, Eastern Kentucky University, The Filson
Historical Society, Georgetown College, Kentucky Historical Society, Kentucky State
University, Morehead State University, Murray State University, Northern Kentucky
University, Spalding University, Transylvania University, University of Kentucky,
University of Louisville, University of Pikeville, and Western Kentucky University.
All rights reserved.

Editorial and Sales Offices: The University Press of Kentucky
663 South Limestone Street, Lexington, Kentucky 40508-4008
www.kentuckypress.com

Library of Congress Cataloging-in-Publication Data

Names: Aldana, Yael Valencia, author.
Title: Black mestiza : poems / Yael Valencia Aldana.
Description: Lexington : The University Press of Kentucky, 2025. | Series:
   University press of kentucky new poetry & prose series
Identifiers: LCCN 2024031919 | ISBN 9781985901230 (hardcover) | ISBN
   9781985901247 (paperback) | ISBN 9781985901261 (epub) | ISBN 9781985901254 (pdf)
Subjects: LCGFT: Poetry.
Classification: LCC PS3601.L34435 B53 2025 | DDC 811/.6—dc23/eng/20240716
LC record available at https://lccn.loc.gov/2024031919

This book is printed on acid-free paper meeting
the requirements of the American National Standard
for Permanence in Paper for Printed Library Materials.

Manufactured in the United States of America.

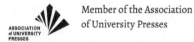

Member of the Association
of University Presses

For my grandmother, Carmen Aldana Valencia,
an abuela lost, then found.

All The Women Are White,
All The Blacks Are Men,
But Some of Us are Brave

—AKASHA (GLORIA T.) HULL,
PATRICIA BELL-SCOTT,
BARBARA SMITH

Contents

III.

IV.

Talisman

I made a new talisman that is both necklace and conjuring.
It is of you, and of them, and of me
   Your initials in scrolled shiny silver rest on my neck.

My Mother,
   your name means blood, namesake, origins.
We are of the Caribbean
   our names mean salt water in the veins,
buried navel strings.
   You are recently dead.
               And what of them?

Ancestors,
   the word means namesakes, origins, blood,
means nothing is lost
   means the Western World, means The New World
which was not new,
         because people were already there.

They have been dead
   dead for centuries
dragged to the bottom of the sea
   on the middle passage in chains
dragged to the bottom of the sea
   for Gold
      for Silver

on the galleon *La Nuestra Señora de Atocha*
   on the Guineaman the *Hannibal*
      dragged out of the green domed
      mountains of Santa Marta, Colombia
      before it was Santa Marta
      before it was Colombia.

I wear their coin around my neck next to your initials
   A coin dredged from their island under the sea,
waterlogged graveyard of   Colombian Gold
      of Caribbean Silver

I wear their coin for ancestors who slipped past
   conquistador steel
   to peer gold rimmed around narrow sloped Santa
   Marta peaks
for the ones that got caught and broke under Spanish yokes
   under British yokes.

I wear their coin for the ones doing the catching
   for those that came from Scotland with money
for those that came from Aldana, Spain, for money
   for those that came from Valencia, Spain, for money
Their riches dragged down into shipwrecked soaked sod-
   den sands
   lost before reaching Spanish coffers
before reaching English coffers
   for me to find and put around my neck.

Mother, no men stay in our family
   they keep on going leaving beautiful dusky sometimes dark
skinned sometimes half-caste children in their wake.

All of you
    curl in my ear,
I will carry you.

Sleep in my Mestiza's body,
    Lay aside the violence that forged this body
my body
    Lay inside my shell of soul and flesh
We are all in here together
    distilled into this one casing of corpuscles.

Sleep in my husk of flesh and soul
    I will carry you.

I.

Una de las Otras [. . .]
They called her half and half.
Mita' y mita', neither one nor the other
but a strange doubling, a deviation of nature
that horrified, a work of nature inverted.
—GLORIA ANZALDÚA

But what if she is more than two parts?

Small Dark and Moving

Open
                    Open
                              I am perverse
I am small dark and moving
                                        I move in waves
I am
                              I am moving rippling
hump my back hump
                    bend my back
            bend
I am fish
      moving under power
                    malachite scales flashing.

Now
                    I transform
I am flower soft
            translucent petals floating on dark
            indigo water
                                        I rise
into air

I want nothing more
                    nothing

inked iridescent feathers stir
    the shadowed avian leaps
        from its branch into
      openness
  pushing up against nothing
      pushing up
          into air.

Black Mestiza

I heard a rumor I didn't exist.
not in your Colombian neighborhood
not in your Cuban neighborhood
not in your Miami neighborhood

because Mestizas are not Black.

a girl just this side of twenty tells me so,
sure of her black wavy haired Latina cred,
born in Miami. her people bred in Colombia.

mi abuela was a proper Mestiza,
from Chinácota, Colombia, in the interior,
almost in Venezuela.
no Black included.

she gained her Black off country.
on twin island shores, bobbing in the Caribbean Sea.
with her Indigenous face and her two thick braids
her passport stamped white
Colombian threads severed.

she gained her Black on Caribbean shores
with my grandfather,
skin black as octopus ink

sheening faintly blue
el Negro.

their daughter as pale as milk
still la Negra
torn from her mother (mi abuela)
vended to an upper-class family
                                in another country.

daughter's skin as pale as milk
                                a currency.
maternal threads severed.
                                Colombian threads severed.

her mother yearning
                                calling to the night for her lost
milk daughter.

                                the threads de mi abuela severed.

I kept my grandmother's face
                                kept the call from her Playa Blanca
                                waters
                                kept the call from her Santa Marta
                                mountains.
                                        kept the call from her Chinácota
                                        forest

the water stretched between us
                                me and her
                                        blood thinned
                                                to filament.

her countrymen call to me,
>> read the code
>>>> of my face
>>>> *¿tu eres Colombiana?*
her country women call me, read the code
>>>> of my face
>>>> *¿tu eres Colombiana?*
>>>> no soy Negra.

Till
>> DNA knit me back together,
>>> us back together
>>>> restored her abuela
>>> fingers in my hair.
>>> from La Negra to her Negra
>>> her fingers though powdered bones
>>> hold still.

>>> in her undertow,
>> with her Indigenous
face and her two thick braids
>> a Mestiza's weight
>>> is not calculated
in blackness
>> but in blood.

Las Mestizas

there is a slip of land on la frontera
a land of haunted untamed tongues
forked and black like the dark.
a land of wild women with smoke cloud
hair and legs that span rivers.
they know how to stand in more
than one place at one time.

I know how to stand in more
than one place at one time.
                              Las Mestizas

they have heard of the Black Mestiza.
they have seen her,   they are her.
they are me.
                                   I am her
jaguar woman's bastard daughter
with Vodun water and a flower
for the virgin's feet
                        Black Mestiza
the Mestiza that winks in and out
del mundo.

they have seen her,   they are her
they are me.
                  we are her.

jaguar woman calls her.
                jaguar woman calls us.
                        the ancestors call her.
                                the ancestors call us.
                                        the ancestors call me.

                                their bones
                                jangling
                                like music.
                        I can feel them moving
                below the water
        that is my skin, crowning at my mouth
a bubble of light that trembles and is released.

we do not care what you think.
                you watch sheenless water.
                        we are not there.
                                look that way
                                and continue to not
                                see us.

you have lost your water and your way.
                you want to take our water from us.
                                you want to take my
                                water from me.

you can never catch us because you cannot see
                                between the waves of the sheenless
                                water.
                                        while you are watching
                                        the surface, we will
                                        crumble into

dust of
la frontera.
I will
crumble into dust
of la frontera.

we will rise into swirling eddies of ash and dirt and sand.
I will rise into swirling eddies of ash
and dirt and sand.
swirl into the mouth of the next
girl child.
swirl into the mouth
of the next boy child.
while you keep
watching the surface
of sheenless water.
while you watch
our bones break fine as sand
we are not there
we are in the mouth of the next boy child
we are in the mouth of the next girl child
we are in the mouth of the next
in-between child.
not beneath
the surface
of sheenless water.

Open Your Mouth

jaguar woman crawls out of the ground,
bone white shells for eyes flashing unseeing
iridescence. open your mouth, granddaughter
bring us, we are waiting, your bone-harrowed
ancestors beneath this soil
Coatlicue exhales her fanged breath over my
goosebumped flesh, her two serpent face so ugly
she was buried twice. open your mouth daughter
breathe in my sinewed avian air. breathe
in my feathered muscled coils spun around your neck.
uncover our plowed-over bones. we are waiting,
call our people out of the mountains, out of rubbled
burned ash piles, out of silted, slimy river bottoms
bring us. we will return to our glinting azure edged shores
dip our feet in fine clear water. hold my yellowed skull
in your hands. open your mouth, clean my teeth
make them yours, intertwine your fingers with us
the terrible women from below this sand.

We Are Very Witchy

Nos estamos haciendo muy brujitas
—SANDRA CISNEROS

We are becoming very witchy
—CISNEROS TRANSLATED BY RUTH BEHAR

we make altars in glittering blue and white mosaics
with plaster skulls and black and white photographs.
we burn candles. we clutch our talismans:
the gold embossed cross around your conquistador neck
the hammered silver cross around your English neck
pictures of stark dour grandmothers
money from absent and dead grandfathers.

ancestors come to the fore
my mother and I call you.
all of you
from your islands beneath my sea.

this is how we burn next to stiff white Anglican prayer
    books
next to Methodist prayer guides with jaunty yellow flowers
next to gold edged Roman Catholic bibles
Ave Maria!
it's still *Coatlicue*. It's still the Oshun
it's still Yagé Medicina. It's still Obeah
it's still Benin Voodoun, clad in crisp white filaments
and wrapped in fire.

Why Don't You Write About Joy?

Why do you keep writing about all this brown girl suffering?

Because when my mother was last pregnant, fate bathed her
    in blood,
they took both her child and her womb though they didn't
    have to.

Because when my grandmother came to the Anglo world,
they cleaved her name in half.

Because my grandmother lost one, then two, then three
children. one to death, one to adoption, one to theft.

Because my mother was torn from her mother and went
    crazy.
Because my grandmother lost her daughter and went crazy.

Because every day, us women on this side of the sea,
though wedded to our cooking pots still make bread.

Because when you want to feel better,
you stand on our necks.

Because we still sing with our faces in the loam.
Because when we have nothing, we still have ourselves.

Because we are still beloved to each other.

Because every night the sun still falls below the ocean
where my people dwell.

Because you cannot hear me
doesn't mean I am not singing.

I Give Different Answers

Those who don't know ask
>*Are you mixed?*
>*Is your father white?*
>*Is your mother white?*
>*What are you then?*
>*Where are you from?*
>*I mean, where are your people from?*

Those who know ask
>*Are you Caribbean?*
>*Which island?*
>We laugh
>We sing the same interloper song.

Those who know ask
>*Are you Colombian?*
>My Spanish professor taught me
>with eggshell white skin
>and hair as dark
>as dreams.
She says, *Eres Colombiana*
>*You are a Mestiza like me.*

Self-Portrait in Your Slices

If their maids speak enough English to understand
—from an anonymous story on the internet

I am the light skinned lighter-than-a-paper bag-one you say
is one of the good ones
I am the dark skinned, 70 percent cocoa one they warned you
     about
I am the octoroon who passes, who you make nigger jokes to
I am the brown cherry wood one you assume is the Nanny
holding my white passing son.
He becomes un-white passing related to me
I can see something in him they say
a darkness they mean
my darkness they mean.
I am the nice brown skinned girl being held by my white
     passing grandmother.
She becomes un-white passing with the context of me
I can see something in her they say
my darkness they mean
her darkness they mean.
I am the throw away character with the funny accent
the best friend to your star.
I add color
the dark kind.
I am Mestiza here in Colombia
I am not a Mestiza there in Colombia
Mestizas are not Black you say.

I am a Black woman, I say

They say, you are not Black
They say, you are not that Black
They say, you are not dark enough
They say, you are not light enough
They say, you are not dusky enough
They say, you are not Black enough.

You are them
They are you.

RE: NI**ER

University undergraduate class: Major American Fiction
Reading list: Flannery O'Connor, William Faulkner
Faulkner writes nigger
O'Connor writes nigger
here
see a nigger, everywhere a nigger
It's not hard to know when you will be niggerized
See: Flannery O'Connor
See: William Faulkner

I am a nigger
The professor is calling me a nigger
The class looks at me,
Brown Girl, he asks
don't you see the beauty,
the amazement of words the craft?
I am a nigger

University undergraduate class: American Literature Masters
Reading: Flannery O'Connor
O'Connor writes pickaninny then nigger
I am a pickaninny then I am a nigger
Brown Girl, don't you see the beauty
the amazement of words the craft?
I am a nigger and a pickaninny

How can I publish anything
if I'm still a nigger and a pickaninny?

University undergraduate class: Writing Fiction
Reading: William Faulkner
page 2 Nigger
Once a nigger always a nigger.
Thank God my son doesn't look like me.
He can pass for a white boy with sparkling
amber eyes.

Angela Davis Was in My Car

I bought new brown leopard patterned seat
covers for my dog chewed interior to drive
her from the college lecture hall to her hotel.

She is redwood tree tall. She walks like a battleship
       cutting through ice.

Her voice fills the car, her sentences trail off
       at the end and keeps on trailing.
Have you heard Angela Davis speak?
her vowels swoop down then curve up and dissipate
       like an Italian, but not like an Italian
like she is from the country of Angela Davis.

I took her to the wrong hotel,
       then to the right hotel.

She was supposed to die in prison
But she didn't. She lived. She lived and rose
lived and took us with her in her rising
kept living, kept on rising
keep on rising, kept on taking us
kept on keeping on
our hands looped around her scarf
threaded through her pockets
our dreams hanging on to her jeans.

I tell her about my classes
tell her, I write about forgotten women
my mother, my grandmothers.
her voice undulates, rolls, ripples
weaves through my mind.

Get on it Girl, she says.

She left three soft steel gray hairs on my head rest
If I had the right incantation
I could make my own
Angela Davis.

Brown Girl

I didn't grow up hating
myself
grew up on my island hearing
You are such a nice Brown skinned girl.
nice Brown
nice skinned
nice girl.
I was nice and Brown
I was nice skinned
I was a nice girl.
Until I came to Brooklyn
I became tough and Black
I became un-nice
imitation of a hard-mouthed
Nuyorican
Brown became bad
Girl became bad
here skin is a problem.

Sister Beloved, Brother Beloved

I will call them my people, which are not my people;
And her beloved and him beloved, who was not beloved.
—ROMANS 9:25

I walk down my sun streaked street
A voice calls,   *Sister?*
I don't know him, but he is mine, of me.

His tone is clear and wanting.
Black man to Black woman.
                              I need you.
I turn
He stands, clipboard in hand, survey-
taking pen ready.

He does not hesitate.
He goes there.
Black man to Black woman
                              I need you.

Sister, I'm standing on this corner, no one is stopping
for me. Is it because I'm a Black man?

I go there
Yes brother, they are young. they are white
you are not of them. They don't see you,

they see through you. They fear you.
I know it.
You know it.

                              But stay.
Be strong. keep on.
We fist bump. I walk on.

They can't know what we have
beneath our hard white shelled eyes.

We, who can call out to a stranger,
and find a sister, and find a brother.

Beloved, we who are not Beloved
to anyone but ourselves.

To Watch the Till Movie

I cannot watch the new Emmett Till Movie
It is me always dying in that river
Me calling and calling for my mother as the life
        is smashed out of me
Me lying in that casket so chewed up my mother
        only knows me by my ring
Me receiving my child's masticated corpse
Me clutching my red beads and a bobbin-lace handkerchief
Me in my black crepe dress
        my face on fire from crying.

My white-passing brother sits on the couch
a promo for the new Emmett Till movie pops
        up on our TV.
He cannot watch.
It's him putting a crisp new suit on his dead, bloated son
        in the most expensive casket
It's still him dying in that car
Him getting his eyes gouged out
Him covered over in the dark airless ground
        in the most expensive casket.
My brother finds my face with his haunted slate blue eyes
He asks, *What would you do if it was me in that river?*
I say, *I would walk out this door into God's sunshine*
        and call and call your name.

Black Person Head Bob

I still count. How many of us are in here?
Five? six? Two, including me?
Why? Are we going to fight somebody?
Our backs against their gilded walls.
Have we made progress?
We made it yet?

If we stare too-too long, sometimes
we head bob.
I see you. You see me.

I see you, a woman on a Philadelphia street
I stare for a half a second too long
You stare for a half second too long
Your houndstooth jacket just so.
Your gray hair just so.
Like my mother would have done.
You see me. We do not speak.
We pass a silent *Go on girl* as we cross.

She is cleaning the university bathroom
in her blue uniform
she sees me. I see her.
We head bob.
We do not speak.
Pass a silent *Go on girl* as we cross.

I ask my colleague, twenty-four to my forty-four
Do y'all still count how many black people are in the room?
Do y'all still hold each other's gaze a half a second too long?
I see you. You see me.
I got you. You got me.
or is that old woman stuff?
old Black woman stuff I learned
from my mother?

I saw you he says. I counted you he says.
I got you. You got me

For our ancestors below the sea
from our ancestors across the sea
I see you, you see me.

Which One Was It?

Which one was it? Which of them that were mine
came shackled in the tiny space too small for a dog,
spitting and moaning and crying, in stench. Them,
too stubborn-strong to die. Them stubborn-strong
enough to live. None from my grandmother's side.
Her women, her mother, her mother, and her mother's
mother, and her mother's mother's mother, and so on and so
on and on and on, tilled slanted viridian hills that became
Colombia. Some brothers, some sisters disappeared
like shifting trees into jagged mountains, impervious
to precious, pious conquistador crosses. They are still there,
peeping out of cracked metamorphic depths. They came
from my grandfather's side, his skin so dark, he's called ink.
They came from my father's side. At least two stacked
like chattel, with cornered-mare fear. They might remain
be faint ink marks, the log of an English pen, a hashmark,
this one and one lived, that one dead, their cool naked fear
in my 2020 eyes.

Zora Neale Hurston

It's not good for people to be forgotten, especially me.
I see y'all come to my grave. I appreciate all the candles
and wine the fake flowers y'all leave I also appreciate that
y'all cleaned up the graveyard so you can see the damn graves.
But what about when I was alive? When I was broke as fuck
in the old persons' home? What about when I was trying to get
my last book published? If it wasn't for that gal, no one would
know who I was. You know her—she wrote that book *The Color
Purple.* I appreciate her story about how she found my grave.
First of all, she didn't fall into some damn hole, and she wasn't
running from snakes. But I'm not mad at her. We writers need
our stories, even if they aren't exactly true. The truth is somewhere
in between. She did pay to get me a headstone. I don't have
the heart to tell her the headstone is not exactly over me.
I'm a little to the left.

The Prettiest Graves

Gather the weight of not having said and place it upon
the prettiest graves
—Joe Wenderoth

which are the prettiest graves?
the ones tended with fresh flowers
Roses, Gardenia, Oleander?
the ones tended with fresh flowers
grass clipped close?
the one with an angel above
weeping languid and crestfallen
bedraggled over the headstone?
are they any more lovely
than the ones with plastic flowers
with the water-stained pictures
the one with an engraved monster truck
the ones lost beneath twisted vines
bowed over grass overgrown
and forgotten?

II.

We Are the Ones We Have Been Waiting For

—ALICE WALKER

Small Dark and Moving: Flying Fish

I am small dark
    and moving
        moving in waves
I am
    I am moving
       rippling
hump my back
          hump
bend my back
      bend

Startled, I leap
    from liquid aqua creamed thickness
        into
           the openness of air
pushing against the void of
         water
     water versus sky.

Eagle Ray

There is a boy, naked, slumped in a white
plastic patio chair, legs twisted around himself.
he was born wrong, his mother says, without
enough oxygen, his mother says, a part of him missing,
his mother says. he slumps on his back porch facing the ocean.
I am there too. His mother hoses him off,
his shower she says. water drips from his slight
folded brown body. to me, she says, *watch him*
to me, his sister's friend, his sister in parts unknown.
the mother leaves the slicked wet porch, eddies
swirl on concrete. Why,
I cannot remember. I cannot watch the boy
in this wretchedness, that his mother would
uncover his smooth unblemished skin fully before
a twelve-year-old girl, his sister's friend, his dignity
flayed. I watch the irregular tumbling surf, now cobalt
blue, now turquoise, now bleach white. Then, he
comes, his form wavering deep brown hugging
sand in shallow water, his darkened body undulates
under his own power, at his own speed. I look
at the boy. Does he see him too? This bay brown
molted slip of a creature, his skin's darkness
punctuated by uniquely white spangles, the chestnut
swooped tips of his wings breaking through viscous
thickness to touch air. The boy's head remains
bowed, eyes turned away, the ray disappears
from our sight.

Hammerhead

I could not imagine that such a creature
could be caught. I could not imagine
the colossal total of his rough hewn weight
or that he could be brought into our world.
A membrane must have been broken, thrust
through to still the muscled breath of this leviathan.
It seemed wrong that three men could labor under
the immensity of his shifting body in shallow water,
in their rickety wooden boat with blue and white
paint peeling, or that my mother and I would
be passing on the road at that exact moment in our
white mini to see his dead king's body and the three
men struggling with him, their prize. How had they
managed it? How had he been taken? Was he hooked?
Or was he found floating, His head slack in death,
fresh still. How had they claimed him? How had they
hoisted him into this shallow pretense of a boat? My
eight year old self wanted to know everything. As usual,
My mother wanted to know nothing. But as usual
she had a story about how she ate shark once
and didn't like it.

Faith Comes at Night
—Tzav, The Zohar

From the red black, blue black
mars black, austere belly of night
she comes along with fear, sparkling
faintly, pressing against all
that could go wrong and does.
when our conviction wavers
drips shadow onto already dark waters,
she is the thread that pulls us
forward wingbeat by wingbeat,
to scratch out secret things
in the heel of the dawn before
the time of muggle work.

why are some of us content
to look up from tunneled darkness
toward a mousehole of light?
she presses us still,   past
bleakness, past barriers. we peel
back each imagined layer of clouded
skin, one by one, to reveal
what is smooth, brown,
and splendid.

Lightning Rod

I could not imagine how I looked
in the parking lot.   a lone figure
vertical in slanting rain,
in the swelling   storm
a future lightning rod
              drops pierce heavy.
my hood goes up.
I scan for my wayward vehicle
it should be easy to see
              red
among the few horizontal
metal hunks left
              scattered.
I turn like a sentinel,
like a lighthouse
mechanical   methodical
clicking and clicking
              and clicking
my key remote
no car.
        it is lost
so am I

              vulnerable,

an opening,   a tender maw.
soft underbelly.
          distracted   ready to be taken
consumed   if someone
          watching   wished it
The only thing that could save me
          is my face
grown in Brooklyn
          as hard as tack.

a white sedan slows.
          I turn, my face hard as tack
          a door unlatches.
I hold my face still, as hard as tack.

it's my friend
          I get in.   we drive slowly
I click. click   click   click

the car breaches where
          where it's always been.
Where I wasn't looking
                    as small,
          as red as ever.
I jump out of her white car
                         into my red
night's weighted water
                    pooling.

Mars Black Night

The lake shines black
a white strip, wide
reflects and ripples,
source unknown
Two girls titter
laughter ebbs
over, under
swinging on their birch seat
Two girls, different girls
in high-waisted pants
one driftwood blue, one lavender lilac
cross me,
stride quickly,
burnished chains clipped to their belts
arc, swinging
A guy in a red fast-food shirt
hustles to his car,
his portable speaker
is aglow, alight,
undulates with thick
jaunty music
A woman glides next to him
in the same uniform
in a red shirt, in black pants
Her eight-month-pregnant belly

uncovered
freed
swaying slightly
unfettered
skin taut and shining.

Sirens

They call from the supermarket newsstand
They call from Instagram, from Facebook

      Hips thrust forward,
                           Concave stomach
              Loins turned inward, Headlines say:
                  Kim,
                        Megan Thee Stallion,

                                      Beyoncé.

Mouths gape silent, parted wanting
        Touch me by the teeth
                I hear them
            my ear a practiced self-hatred.
        They say
            want me,
                  touch me
                      be me.
                    Touch me by the
                            teeth.

    say
    this is female-hood
            femaleness,   womanhood
                womanness

                    Lips parted   slightly
                    breathe,
                                barely
                                    just
                                        just enough.

Suck it in,
        liver cleanse,
                detox tea, lose twenty pounds
                        in two weeks.
                            Eat   just barely,
                                    not   enough.

            A better version of you
                    revenge body
                        make them look
                            you know you
                                you know they

                                            want it.

I listen   pick my wallet
                                pick my bones.

        Make us richer

I dash my head against their rocks.

Nothing left of me
        but them.   Smiling
                filterized
                        those
                            who   do   not   exist.

The Hoot of a Hobnail

It's an abject amalgam of an anomalous and austere nature. That we although, both belligerent and baleful are much beribboned. We are a cadre, a clamber of craggy, doleful yet doggedly dour and dubious dyads. Everyone knows that the best ersatz for eminence is both forlorn and furtive. Although the glean of a hobnail is both hunkered and hardy but hemmed in hackles that are hewn are a hoot. Whether inert, impassive, or incongruous, it's as if the judicious and the jaunty become larval in the loam. We meander mournfully though a myriad of modulated and noteworthy but nebulous and obtuse pallid perches. Although sometimes more prosaic, petulant, and placid to quell the ruminative, rueful, and the rank. We suffused the scions with taciturn, unwieldy, unworthy, yet unwaveringly visceral, viscous wattles. And untimely we warily waylay the wavering and the wan. Xenomorphs, beware of the Xenophobic, the yapping yawl of a Yarborough yeoman, and the zippy zero-sum zingers of zealotry, Zarathustra's zenith.

When Margaret Atwood Meets My Dead Professors

These are nice words here.
This is a good poem
I'll make a pencil mark, a note,
I'll underline
but then there is Margaret
my hitch, my crux, my latch
she's the one that's that catch in between
the flotsam to my jetsam.

She goes together with him, that professor,
Hal with his one skinny leg on the desk
with the sock in the clogs.

With him, I thought the world could be changed
I was fresh, unspoiled like a pomegranate. I thought
people would listen to me. like he did.

When someone dies you replay their memory
So you don't forget. they change
each time
every time.

They are all dead.
My professors

him too skinny leg always with the jeans
and the patterned socks and the clogs.
Bill ambling with the duck shoes and the
too busy sweaters. Arthur with the side
swagger and the chinos.

You all didn't need to be so good
should have warned me about men, the other kind.

Maybe I should have stayed there nestled
up that hill, with socked, clogged
sweatered men. never to meet
the ones with cruel downturned eyes.

Margaret is still alive. I want to be a moment
a cog in the endless line of her wheel.

I want to be that woman she
remembers with the chinoed, socked,
sweatered professors behind my eyes.

To Be Margaret

Oh to be you, to have two sparkling
scrunched-up eyes, one wolf brow
higher than the other, looking like you
know more than you should, not caring
if you don't.

I want to be unafraid and clean the back
of my stove with sunflower yellow gloves
with my adult son and put it on Instagram
like you.

I want to shrink admirably like you,
nurse a still smaller mother, unfurling
wisdom like bits of fern, rancid
with knowledge.

I want to talk about growing up during
The war, like you.
For some, there was only one war
World War II.

Those were my parents, not me.

Did you eat lots of liver like they did?
Because that's all the meat there was?

Did you learn to stand your ground
like they did?
Do not move.   Do not yield.
To die on that mythical hill
for country, for family.
it doesn't matter the war
is seventy years gone.

The veterans of liver
austerity and made up hills
are falling away
falling off this planet.

Will I meet you before you tumble
off this earth? Can we talk about ferns
and liver and wolves?

Cisneros Is a Name

but also a word that can be used
to mean anything.
The snow cone man arrives,
his truck rotting at the seams
He calls out *Come gets your Cisneros.*
$1 each.
I get cherry
flavor with condensed milk.
Red syrup flows, staining
tiny white ice chips. La sangre
of this man sweating all day
for treats a dollar each

Damned Cisneros. I yell
as I stub my toe on the bed post.
My son comes up with that he-
wants-something-look-on-his-face!
I tell him
Boy don't try my Cisneros
He walks away huffing frustration
The food truck vendor in the ole
town park asks me, how do you want
your Cisneros? Extra crispy, I say.
I open this book that says
Cisneros on the cover

and it gets me through.
People say she's old and established
I say she answered me on Instagram
once with a whole sentence
I can die happy with that.

Spanglish to Spanish

I know she's horrible,
I know she would take the food
out of my mouth, out of your
mouth, out of my son's mouth
but I love her. I love her because
she's old, I love her because
she reminds me of my
mother my grandmother

who died old. We work together,
behind the fancy jewelry
counter at Bloomingdales
in Aventura, Florida.

When she sees you waiting on a customer
she turns like a listing battleship
a wounded bull
she waves you off with a flick
of her tree-knotted hands
That's my customer, she'll say.

Every customer is hers even
if she has never seen them before

Her-better-than-you-because-you-are-but-dust-beneath-
    her-feet-Cuban-accent,
makes her English sound like Spanish,
ballad of a husky nightingale.

She makes me want to turn my Spanglish
into Spanish

I show her my book Isabelle Allende's
La Isla Bajo El Mar. She says,
Niña, let me see.

She takes it. Then, sees a customer.
She lurches over, leans in to her prey,
to close her sale   but then steps
back, slightly nods her head to me
yields the customer.

She gives me the easy sale she has primed
I won't tell anyone, so she can keep her reputation
The shark in our water.

Susanna returns to the stool at my station
sits like a toad and reads the book she
has stolen from me.

Edgar Suite

1. *Return to Chinácota, Colombia*

I want to go to Chinácota, Colombia, where
my grandmother is from, where she was born
in the Colombian interior, almost in Venezuela.
But I am afraid the FARC will clap their hands
on my back, jut a rifle cold to my chin, buddle me
into their wet mountain lairs, for green backed money.

I could explain my government won't pay
anything for me, won't pay anything for a Black
American Immigrant, won't pay anything to a Blonde
bleached Black American. My government, who
is happy to let Black souls die for nothing

I want someone to protect me. A bodyguard,
my friend, the biggest person I know,
The biggest Venezuelan, Edgar.

A champion body builder 6' 1", 262 pounds.
As big as Arnold was. As big as Arnold wishes he were again.

Spanish is Edgar's mother language. He can help me
read brittle timeworn records, turn yellowed worm
eaten pages with his muscular fingers. Read the ink
my Spanglish cannot understand. Read to me why

my grandmother left her forest for unknown
Caribbean shores with nothing,
not even her language.

Would we be more obvious to the FARC?
The biggest Venezuelan and the Blonded
Black American, asking questions about
a woman long dust?

Would we be like a Matador's muleta? Pieces of red
fabric waving, fodder for the FARC? The biggest
Venezuelan, The bleach Blonde American
Immigrant prey animals.
Come and get us.

2. The Biggest Venezuelan

I see him next to a Carrara marble Hercules,
at the Metropolitan Museum of Art, on their Instagram.

he's bigger than Hercules, all muscles, all sinew, all girth,
The biggest Venezuelan, Edgar.

I click follow. I follow him.

he's an artist. he paints pictures of Gaia swathed
in vermilion, of Zeus outlined in Phalo blue,
Hera bathed in alizarin crimson.
I am one of thousands that follow
his muscles, his sinew, his girth
his brush.

he notices me.

maybe because I post more than emojis.
maybe because I write phrases.
I write sentences.

He says things to me like, friends,
te adoro amiga, my love.

I say to him, why me. ¿por qué yo?
I say to him, don't you see a bleach Blonde la Negra?
bottom of the Latina hierarchy,
when you are at the apex?

he says, like Austen's Darcy
I see a see a pair of fine dark eyes.
he says, like Austen's Darcy
I count time in eras.

Una de mis mejores amigas.

Por siempre.

3. Por Siempre

I wish I could inhale you, to ingest
your body that fumes iridescent
and dangerous. I would risk ambered
immolation to feel how you live,
on stardust, on our furrowed brows,
on our bleated prayers,
how the gods live,
as if.

I've never been so well-regarded
by such dark eyes, my name (meaning
honey bearer), never so well-cradled
on a breath.

they have marooned you here,
for us to contemplate, to observe
to regard. I turn you over on my tongue
rub you against my teeth. the trick
is to go beyond your storied body.
to dare the penumbra of your thousand
fathom eyes, to touch your lightest web,
amorphous, still sticky.

when the leaves fall dry and weighted
among your too muscled fingers
who will tend to you?

wasn't I the first one to suckle you among
the milkweed on Mount Eryx?

I was your first, maybe not your only
but also your last Melissa.

III.

It is the most tapered kind of affection . . .

Rodrigo Suite

1. For You

There was a time
in the pantheon
the time before quasars
the time before penumbras
were invented
the time before souls
when we were twins clung together
brothers? sisters?
who knows, but one skin
one gossamer bubble
of thread, dark eye to dark eye.
the residue adheres
sticky filaments on the wing
it arrows, it winnows
stretches thin as mylar.
it is the most tapered
kind of affection.

2. Remembering the Future on North Miami Ave

you write me a note in a book
on its crisp unread pages
with your too thick fingers
you didn't know it then,
but I know it now
Para Mi Yael
your City is my City
which means you will go
where I go.

with a Jack and Coke in your left hand
you touch the fingers of your right
to my skin, make new
typography of my body.
arm, thigh
hand
back again
arm   thigh . . .

you say something to the person
on your right
but turn my way.
put your shark eyes on me
put your sharp hand on me

put your soft fingers on me.
I close that book
I forget.

you didn't know it then
what your fingers remembered.
but I know it now.

3. Aquarius Sun, Leo Rising, Virgo Moon

his affection holds like
still water, silver rivulets
flashing by metaled fish
in cool dark depths.
he is still there even when absent.
a ghost, like two pollen-filled
breezes stacked together. when
you need him, curse him for his
empty air, curse him because
you want him
close to you,
he is there, thick shagged hair
wedged under an army green hat.
he says
yes you can do it.
yes I love you.
yes I'm busy.
and he is gone again.
his absence
a type of presence.

4. Amado de mi Alma

Give me this
—ADA LIMÓN

If there was a pill, maybe red, liquid, thin,
rubbered membrane, or maybe orange, oval,
and smooth, or maybe white and chalky
that would sever the nexus between us,
I would throw it down my moist peached
maw. He too, would pinch it between his
potato farmer fingers, muscle it dry across
his tongue, sideways down his throat. Greedily,
take it to be rid of me. We are all eye rolling,
all lip curling, sneering resistance to any,
to all peace. We cannot stand each other.
But we love each other. In this quiet, his dry
warm skin becomes mine. When in proximity
his chest opens, a galaxy. My universe spins
into his. All hot plasma. We are luminous
gas giants winking on and off, moving past
moving into one darkness.
                              lighted cold fusion.
He purses his lips as if to say no, we cannot
escape this gravity. I point with my chin
as if to say yes, we have lured each other here.
He lifts his dark-dark eyes to mine, as if to say,
No, we cannot escape this singularity.

Stay with Me
a Lia Purpura Cento

In this way I begin to speak to him.,
slant and sidelong. It traveled jittery
over the wrinkles of his forehead.

                              Stay with me.

Events will fit themselves to themselves.

                              Stay with me.

Something alighting, something bestowing.

Was I awaiting some sign of passage?
Did I expect, finally, the solemnity
of procession? the strains of ceremony?
Not the hair braided by some woman's
hands, her knuckles hard against his head,
death gowned and dancing.

                              Stay with me.

I lived days as a crouch. everything
cropped, in focused, contained,
naked, looked through and turned inside
out and found lacking. How even as I twisted

free, I wanted to be caught, know the dip
of bone and hammock of skin.
How what seems in the end *inevitable*,
is a trail of particulars finding each other.

The tiny stiff hairs that made nets to catch me.

The Necromancer Returns in Distress

I have never made love
for comfort before
my clothes come off like
wet tissue in your hands
the soulmate fire gone
slim hips to slim hips
it is love still.

your voice vibrates
hummingbirds in my ear
I laugh.
we look like we are in love.
we are not
but we love still
I don't want to go to the late
nite BBQ place
I go
your hand warm, low
on my back.
we have never been
so easy
our knives sheathed.

dawn's tangerine clouds
bring a new month.

I watch you drive away
in your blood orange SUV.
free.
I walk under the pink
plumeria tree to my yellow door
free.
love still.

Single Strand

The pull of a smooth
single strand of hair
beneath my watch strap
reminds me of your coils
I find cooly tangled
in my fingers
after you are
well gone.

Taurus Sun, Taurus Moon, Virgo Rising

I recoil.
when she reaches for me,
                    Her touch
motherly.   The brush of her
fingers foreign.
The stubby fingers that held
similar affection, dust for 17
years, in a Lakeland cemetery.

when I fall, she catches me
by the wrist
forgets I am a mother
forgets I am the family pack
mule   driven by coffee
and will
reminds me I am human
reminds me my feet were once
small and kicked under maternal
fingers.
reminds me the world will still
be there   bleating demands
after I take a nap.

Virgo Sun, Pisces Rising

I have decided she is part angel
We have decided.   Not just me,
more than one of us.   She has been
gifted to us   Maybe she
can't escape back to the silvered walls
of heaven   Forced to stay
here with us rabble.   Maybe
for stealing a frosted cupcake off God's
table.   Forced to stay
here with us,   Her fingers
long and fine clutching imaginary pearls
fingering life's-crushing slights
                      Her voice nightingale
clear   Her pain hidden
by fine eyes, a light voice an easy laugh
She deflects   but gives
us, her students'-selves to ourselves.
She's borne raw in her writing,
Her spider-jittery   handwriting
ragging, witty,   piercing,
her words peer back   at us
eyes unhooded
and   unflinching.

To Watch Her Face Fall

I

I am wounded
my washi thin skin darkens with blood
frayed open flesh ragged
at the edges. I don't want
to tell her, to show her—
but she will ask.

I can bear it alone, the weight of this upset, knit
the lesion back before I see her,
continue the interlacing of fascia after
I see her, conceal the bruise
the sliced skin—
but she will ask.

I harrow then sear watching her face crest and fall
watching her shining shadow. If only for a few
minutes till her face brightens,
till her mouth dances to distract
from my harm.

Our love is this silent chaffing.

II

Bodily harm becomes invisible shadowing
barely darkened imperfections, a closing
over that will smooth—
return to unblemished perfection
to all eyes but ours, only us aware
of the slight scar lightly covered in hair.
Smoothing over her face that fell.

She cannot forgive because it was me
I cannot forgive because it was her—
her face that fell.

She wants to go back. Soothe
with words as slim as apple chips.
Soothe with her rhythmic voice
that rises and falls in waves.

Our faces slick over, leaving only slight
sharpening in the corners of the shields
in our eyes squinting, glinting
black metal.

She will say it's alright and not mean it
I will agree and not mean it.

We will put our glossy heads together,
draft new plans for unnamed streets.

She will hold my hand tighter
which is the only good bit. Until I am ready
to leave the hearth of her protection
sheathed in armor we will temper
anew.

Nameling

I want to be her nameling
her name twin exactly the same,
but if I can't have her whole
I want a part a bit of, some
of, some extraction of
                    Marie

Donna Marie, Julie Marie.
It's the sound of the word,
the name   Marie
first, low rumblings of earth
then the sharp uptick of light
at the end
                    Marie.

Melissa Marie would be good.
But I left that name, long ago
let it float away like the wiles
of honeybees, let it float away
with its unkind origins.
                    Melissa,
named for a girl no one liked,
her bad luck sticking like taffy

When I called my Donna,
Donna Marie, people would say,
why do you call her that? I would
say because that's her
name.

Dear Sociopath

I know you well. The woman that gave birth
to me, but is not my mother is of your kind.
I feel sympathy. I know as a child you went
through things, terrible things. You   separated,
your feelings fled, so you would   not feel
the full clench of adult hands on your spider
thin neck. I know I am now an object   to you,
to dominate and command.   I understand
that you do not feel. Your soft warming
thoughts waned and died,   boxed and left
uncovered in singed heat. That feeling child
died beneath broad adult fingers.   I understand
you only imitate emotions and   that you
are very good, but   like all imitators,   you make
mistakes.   I know   the feel of you,
the touch of you,   a practiced sense from my own
childish lessons. Unlike you   I feel too much,   feel
your cool sapphire heart muscle. And as   you would do
to me, I put you in a box, cover you over,   Label you:
not to be played with,   make you an object—
a translucent   aquamarine cube
            do   not   touch.

I soften
after Julie Marie Wade

I soften away from the man
at my editing job who tells me.
It is your reaction to perceived disrespect
that is the problem. There is no disrespect.
It is my problem, not his problem,
my problem.
I soften, I bend away, let him fall
away from him like dry fall leaves
rustish red, marigold yellow, blood
beneath the skin purple.

I soften I soften

My son's anxiety rushes at me
needle fine
targeted,
directed at my solar plexus
he is collapsing. I must fix him,
fix me
fix me, mother. I am dying
in this moment, I am dying
I know I am not dying, but I am dying.

I, am angry. I, am busy.
Why is there no wife to soothe

Me, His mother? I look for her
Oh yeah,   she doesn't exist

I soften I soften

Remind him of the ancestors beyond
the veil. Remind him Granny is always
watching. Remind him he is the best boy
with the one curl in the middle of his forehead.
Remind him his Granny will come in his
dreams to tell him so.

My student tells me, I am old. My student tells
me I am not a Latina because I don't speak
Spanish. My student tells me my Spanglish
is an invalid gringa nightmare. I think about
snapping her head off, snapping her teeth out.
cutting through her knees with a Brooklyn
comeback.

I soften I soften

I tell her she has a pretty name
That like hers, my grandmother came
from Colombia.
That like hers, my grandmother came
with two squat braids,
no English, and a tight smile.

I soften I soften.

Stuyvesant Ave Bodega

The dust colored, comma shaped
cat lays languid, across the freezer,
so I can't get to the Häagen-Dazs bars.
The new sour candy nerds are jumbled
behind the old ones. Minerva the Nuyorican
with skin like a wadded paper bag likes
when you pay in quarters. Her youngest son
Juan with eyes the color of honey, hits
on us junior high girls when we stop
in afternoons, wants to know if we are going
to use our bras as pooper scoopers
for the dog wandering by. We don't answer.
His older brother Filipe, as tall and as thin
as a cattail, knows our breakfast orders
by heart. He slaps them on the counter
three at a time, *three coffees light and sweet.*
three egg ham and cheese on an everything bagels
When he's in a good mood he winks. He calls
my mother Mrs. C. Tells her, he's brought her
the good milk from the back. Minerva asks
us what we are learning in school. Asks us
if we have reached the Roman pantheon.
Asks us if we know she was named
for a Goddess.

The F Train 1999

I feel the whoosh, hear the rumble,
I taste a gale of tepid air
I can't make it, no way
No chance
I'm too far up the outside steps
I run anyway
Swipe my metro card, run,
Crook my bag under my arm, run
Thunder down the steps, run
at the right cadence, run
Two steps at a time, run
I can't make it
scramble for the last car, run.

A wheat colored Timberland boot
pierces the silver line
of the closing doors.
I sail though steel toe cracked air
A head bob the only thanks needed.

Carlito

I want my father to be Carlos a Nuyorican
                 Not some guy from Canada I never met who
                 shows up in the crescent of my adulthood.

I want a father who has a panther tattoo inked on his horse
         neck that reminds him of Curtis Sliwa.
                 Not a guy who tells my brother he wants me
                 to text him first.

I want a father who tells the story that he wasn't ready to be
         my father, who stayed drunk on tequila for two days.
                 Not a guy armored with excuses why he
                 wasn't around. Me he just found out about,
                 my brother he ignored for 40 years.

I want a father the neighborhood guys call Carlito although
         he's as big as a Buick, who I call
         Papa Carlito behind
         his back, who says don't call me Carlito I'm your
         father.
                 Not a guy so known by this nickname no one
                 remembers his legal name
                 not my brother,
                 not my first cousin.

I want a father who worked as a bike messenger after I
            was born, was the fastest thing on two
            wheels,
            who at night went to work after hours at Jesus'
            neighborhood autobody shop till
            Jesus took him
            on full time, till he became a partner, till he took
            over the business.
                        Not a guy who waited for five years to reach
                        for me after he found out
                        I existed.

I want a father who cries when he's drunk saying he should
            have stayed with my mother
            who wouldn't have him.
                        Not a guy that got two women pregnant
                        at the same time.

I want a father who pretends he wasn't crying when his three
            daughters graduated from college
            because he didn't
            graduate from high school.
                        Not some guy that didn't know I went to
                        college at sixteen.

I want a father who met me at the corner by the bodega
behind my mother's back, who buys me
            the gold
            doorknocker earrings she forbids and lets me,
            and my friends hang out in front
            of his auto shop and talk shit.
                        Not a guy I think is dead when my brother
                        says he has news of our father.

I want a father that yells at me because I speak Spanglish not
       Spanish, who doesn't consider himself
       Caribbean
       because he's Puerto Rican. It's a different planet
       he says.
              Not a guy who doesn't remember my mother,
              doesn't know her from Eve.
              Who when I show
              him a picture of her thinks she is me.

This Afternoon

I mainly think about what I
will eat next, sharp cheddar
on well-toasted sourdough
my next cup of coffee
always espresso. whether
I will add chocolate syrup
how much work I have.
avoiding that work, doing
that work. about the dog
is she happy? about my
son. how did he come to be?
about my Mother? where
has she gone?

IV.

more than once.
i have the bones you hardened
and built daughters
and they blossom and promised fruit
like afrikan trees.
—LUCILLE CLIFTON

Small Dark and Moving: Black Bird

Open
        Open
                I am not
        perverse
I am small dark and
                        moving
                I am moving in
        waves
                        I am
        I am moving rippling
Hump my back
        hump
                Bend my back
                        bend
        I am a fish
                I am a flower
        soft petals
                Am now.
                I want nothing more
I think of nothing
                else but
the stirring of a
                shadow bird
        as it leaps from its
                        hearth

          into openness
pushing
         up from
                  air.

Titan

You couldn't know that when dealing
with the Titan that you become one yourself.
You are but a girl. Your weapons, rolled
eyes behind the slip of her back. An impassive
you-just-don't-care face. You don't feel
how strong your bones grow beneath the litany
of her couched warnings. Her world is dangerous,
flashing red deadly. Her pointed fingers caution,
cajole, admonish. Watch out for the neighbor
in the billowing yellow dress, the gray cross-eyed
cat. You ignore her, you sigh. Then, those you know
say you are iron-willed to her iron-forged. You
glimpse your own cajoling finger.

Sweet and Low

As I grow older and less stupid
she creeps into my bones
silent and warm, my love solidifies.
I watch her while making the tea
she will soon request.

It's 7 p.m. Jeopardy is on TV.
She is chomping furiously
on chicken, stabbing her index
finger at the air. Shouting wrong
questions at frazzled contestants.
Who is Karl Lagerfeld?

She used to drive me crazy.
With her tended cloud of short
gray curls, the rhythmic circling
of her fingers while she waited.

She calls me. She thrusts her almost
empty plate in my direction, chicken
bones chewed into dust.

Bring my tea Girl. Don't forget my Sweet and Low.

I haven't forgotten in thirty years.

Sixteen years on and all that's
left of her are knickknacks
on a shelf.

A few pink packets are tucked
on my bookcase. Her grandson
chews his chicken bones
into dust.

Nineteen

My fish glides silently in his fish world. I watch him undulate; he is more lovely here in my mother's house than in my grim dorm room, among its antique particle board furniture. He flashes steely green, silver, vermilion. A breeze through the living room windows stirs long ivory lace curtains over his tank. They lift silent, their bodies flap, then drift down and are still. Out of sight, my mother, with her gray-rimmed brown eyes, rustles a paper bag with her laundry. It is a bright practiced sound. She stands between me and life and death and poverty and the terror of my youth. She does it well. She does it alone. She has done it before. We move together through this verdant wonderland full of leaves turning brown and dangerous, small furred animals, and other desperate teenagers. My two older sisters have disappeared into adulthood. Outside, the light shimmers in dappled circles on the ground.

Haiku

My mother, protecting me from life,
small woman, inconsequential
walking down the street.

My Mother and I Save Our Yogurt Containers to Reuse Them

We people are part of the dirt and loam
of the wet between the toes. This, our sun,
prickles our skin. An ancient return of the bones
formed from old habits. We are inconvenient.
Not plastic parts blooming and becoming
filler of this aching body we call Earth. This
is a calling. We are a net, small dots winking
in and out. This is not of convenience, not
in comfort. We stretch wide and thin
across this dream that is both thin and deep,
red-black and yawning as a moonless night.
We have no humility. We sniff and point fingers
at the Styrofoam cup in your hand. Sleeping
and dreaming of a body consuming so much,
to burst the web, of never having enough
of everything. If only to taste the blood.

Grief in Pink Double Pantoum

My grandmother startled me by dying
when told I sat blinking unknowing
trapped in far away in a country supposedly
on vacation, a country of green money
       and bright yellow plastic.

I sat blinking unknowing when told
because my mother believes in shielding children
on vacation in countries of green money
       and bright yellow plastic
She forgets the uncomfortable tight
       fingers of youth's ache.

I sat blinking now knowing a new sharp strangle
       of pain.
I remember everything.
My mother forgets the uncomfortable tight
       fingers of a child's ache.

Supposedly Granny disappeared
       underground
in a scrubbed linen shroud
beneath wet loamed earth.
I did not see her go. I looked at her new dark
       earth, bed puzzling

looking for her scrubbed linen shroud.
Her old bed crisp and empty
I did not see her go. I looked at her new
       dirt bed puzzling.
Her old bed still covered in the flowered sheets she liked

still crisp and empty.
I could understand gone. But where?
from her old bed covered in the flowered
       sheets she liked
It couldn't be in that graveyard

as lovely as it was
with its heavy dark ferns swaying
next to Granny TeTe.
Besides, she couldn't die

slip beneath this world with its dark ferns swaying.
She couldn't breathe under there.
And besides she couldn't die
She is somewhere unknown strumming
       strings in her pink house coat.
Because she had to be still breathing out there,
wishing good-as-gold dreams to everyone,
somewhere unknown, strumming, shimmering
       strings in her pink housecoat.

Besides, Granny couldn't die.
Because if she could die, then my mother could die.
And if she died, then this shifting golden
       world would spin off its axis.
With its paper money and bright yellow plastic.

The Queen's English

My mother decided I cannot be out of her sight
We traversed the uneven cobbled
driveway of a McMansion to deliver
a crisp black package, expensive jewelry
no one needed.
A fortyish woman
her hair an aggressive frizz opened the door.
Her eyes settled on my elfin mother.
Does she speak English? She asks.

There is a small shifting movement
from the elf like a leaf bending to rain.
I knew she would rise from her sleeping depths,
my mother I knew from before.

Her voice strong, singsong but sharp said,
I speak the Queen's English.

I looked at my wisp of mother. She is glaring
indignant. I handed the now-bewildered
woman her package.

We reached the car. Her eyes returned
to softness, uncertain. Dementia has taken
her back. *Can we have Chinese for dinner?*
she asks. I nod yes. She has already forgotten
her elegant fuck you.

My Mother's Advice

Always roast a chicken
on Sundays. It will keep
through the week

I know how to roast
a chicken with rosemary
and butter under the skin,
curry chicken is better. You
always used too much
paprika, leftover poultry
frozen in day-glow
Tupperware.

A houndstooth suit
is perfect in all occasions
and better with a strand
of long pearls.

Not really but I have one
just in case. The jacket looks
better with jeans or linen
pants. Probably looks best
in the closet.

Every woman should
own a red lipstick
Revlon's Cherries
in the Snow works
for everyone.

Red lipstick is full
of confidence when I have
none, a hard bit mouth
disguises all emotions.

If I lived I would
be the same age
as the Queen.
"Rule Britannia" is the best

I remember—I can sing a
"Rule Britannia" high C—like
you, make the cat's ear
twitch. The Queen is dead

song I sing. Do you
remember?

I miss you.
I need you.

Remember people need you
You don't need them.

I need people. I need you.
You never told me you
loved me. Never made me
fresh chocolate chip cookies
like a real American Mom
I didn't need to hear it.
I knew.

When you are in trouble
call me.
I can get there faster
than before.
I can do more than before.
Tell that to my Boy
my grandson.

I make him fresh chocolate
chip cookies like a real
American Mom
I know
he knows.

Mother's Eyes

Her eyes are brown. Irises rimmed in gray—
light gray. This happens sometimes
when Black people get old.
What would I give her?
A wildflower?
A kiss?
I give her
          these things.

What would I do for her?
Would I brush her raven black hair?
Would I carry her mango
laden grocery bags?
I do these
          things already.

What would she do for me?
I want to say anything, but she wouldn't.
She has lots of rules, lots of limitations.
But she would die for me.
She would perish
where she stood
to protect me
          her daughter.

She will never die
and neither will I.
We will be together
forever.

She did die.

                But we are still together.

November 6, 2006, Pompano Beach

My feet shiver on the warm froth edged sand of this Florida
    Beach.
My mother is gone, disappeared into an urn
in black granite clad niche.

Will I walk into the storm of this gray-blue water?
Struggle for each bitter breath, let rage be ripped
from my lungs, Then, drift away peacefully.

Mother, you said we are people
of the sea and the loam.
How can I remain in this world
without your   eyes holding
me in it?

The cerulean water of our tropical island
is different, glassy and placid, leviathans turning just
beneath. Mother, we have never been to the beach
together in this country.

It was you who said
if you have a cold, have a sea bath
If you are coughing too much
have a sea bath. If you are not coughing
enough, have a sea bath.

You didn't go.
Is that why you died? You forsook the sea
you broke our ocean's code.

Did it cull you? taking you back into its blue-black depths?

I step into a burgeoning pool, sink to my ankles.
I must stay because of your grandson
your Boy   my Boy.

He is tucked into my third floor
apartment. Face probably thrust out an open window
yelling down at the parking lot ducks
while his father hovers, filming everything.

Did I die that November day?
Did I walk into that churning ocean and drown?
Only the gravity of my boy's amber eyes,
now seventeen prove
I lived.

Houndstooth Suit

If it was up to me, you would have been buried
in it. This most powerful version of yourself.

Bette Davis could have worn it in the forties
in one of her man-eating movies.

Is that where you saw it, Mother? Your first houndstooth
suit? In a murky, shrouded theater, black and white shadows
leaping on the screen over a black and white checkerboard
pattern that is not quite a checkerboard pattern? Or

did you see one on the streets of Brooklyn? Encircling another
beauty when you were there studying your hairdressing course?

I saw a woman on my street, clad in houndstooth pantsuit,
red, irreverent patent leather stripes down each leg.

I thought of you spinning in your urn with disapproval.

She looked as good as you did—As I do. As every woman
armored in dog teeth, a shield to life's bitter wind.

Rebuilding Mother

In the dark of my closet, a wool skirt suit
hangs, not mine, heavy, a person watching.
A hairbrush with her hair still in it lives
in my top dresser drawer, along with her never
worn scarves, the-too-good-for-every-day-real-gold-
dangle-earrings, a small ceramic bell inscribed
with October
(her birth month) sits atop the bookshelf
on the shelf below, her too thick bifocals perch
atop a gold rimmed Roman Catholic bible.

This is what is left.

I stamp my foot in the smoke of ancestors
I say the right obeah incantation,
She rises fully formed, ironclad
her crooked finger thrust out
to criticize my overcooked chicken.

The suit goes into storage, the hairbrush goes
into the garbage, the glasses remain. I use them
sometimes to read too tiny text.

When the 2016 election starts to go wrong
my son puts them on his nose.

Can Granny fix the election? He asks.
Not even she can do that I tell him.

He ignores me, falls asleep with them askew
on his head, praying to the dead for absolution.
In the morning, he wakes, a convex lens
broken little boy reverie
ravaged.

Inheritance

memory the beauty of body
my mother's, my aunt's, my sister's
I now inhabit. middles burgeoning
with middle age, mackintosh shaped
panza included, thickening legacy
of a misplaced grandmother.

the memory of this body is supposed
to be sad, handed down, plied
with desperation to remain shadowy
gleaning slim, gleaning sexy
from the side of a toxic cleanse box.

this wasteland of a body, my body
this memory curveballs, still true,
into newborn promise every morning.
unhemmed by Facebook ad
expectations. I jiggle my panza like
a brand new toy.

From the Stupor of Illness
after Margaret Atwood

I emerge
as if from illness.
blinking,
in demi-silence,
aside my meals
of chicken fricassee
mashed potatoes.

as if I am still young
my mother comments
on my pallor
while
my father tells me useful
but uninteresting things.

Tuesday Morning

The bed holds me, with heavy warm
fingers. My son stirs there is a clattering,
a smashing.
he is angry at me his mother.
I have said no to what he wants.
he is a seventies dream
big earth-wind-and-fire hair
a scraggly Jim Morrison beard.
square jawed, more thirty-three
than seventeen.
body too big to house
his little boy dreams. he rages.
He aims a clear heavy
drinking glass, smashes
the base of the toilet

his ire blooms and is spent.

when I uncurl my toes into this bright
morning air, things will need to be done.
the dog needs to be fed
coffee frothed
for now, reality recedes
distant
fifteen minutes more until my slippers
will crunch porcelain
and I need to corral a baleful imp.

Legacy

They tell me right to my face. *Your*
son, he looks nothing like you.
They see your photo.
Benevolent, head tilted
over my bookcase.

Ah, he looks just like his Granny.

He's seventeen now and you
dead, sixteen years since.

I know you return to him
at night, whispering near his corkscrew
curls, tell him that he is the king
of all he sees, that he is not a boy
but *the Boy.* Because he is

Granny's boy.

His amber eyes settle on me.
He wants something
and he will have it. He is
like you, terrible
same steady gaze, same sun
shining out of his face.

But we are lucky.
You teach him to be kind
to us, your subjects now his.

You made him yours
down to the bones
as you did me.

The Sea

My son no longer swims in the ocean.
He no longer goes to the beach.
He is afraid of sharks.
He feels their grayed-shadowed forms
all teeth, all stealth, burgeoning beneath the waves
snapping off his feet.

This is the Atlantic, an official ocean
Mother, ours is the Caribbean, a Sea
Sea, which means smaller, some say lesser.
Smaller than the ocean.
Lesser than this ocean.

I still go sometimes. I believe what you told me,
that it is our mother, that I am its daughter,
that a sea bath cures all. I still go

for you. Because you remain in her swells,
formless and nebulous like albumin
pulling apart, coming together
like sargasso.

The sargassum piles high now at the shore
stinking.
There is too much fertilizer coming off the coast
of Brazil. the Caribbean Sea is choking with this gulfweed's

long-browning tendrils, sending rotting rogue
sargassum to Florida coasts. They feel like
sharks in the water, dark,
slowly moving.

Only you, Mother, learned how to turn seawater into blood
how to turn sargassum into hope. You never told me how
think of the lives you could have saved
turning saline
into plasma.

I hear your voice
       carried in currents' *troughs:*

Girl Please, It's seawater not saline,
and they are too lazy to collect it properly.
They would destroy the beach, destroy the land,
destroy the fish, destroy the people.
They will die stupid.
Leaving us old women who know everything
with our cooking pots.
They would kill more than are saved.
The sea will take them back.
She is benevolent.
I am not.

After, us grandmothers will come out with
those under our protection and start again
like my Boy, your Boy.
He'll be the first man to stay in our family.
He's stupid now, but don't worry.
I am watching. His amber eyes will change
and turn to meet us old ladies in the sea.

Acknowledgments

With gratitude to the editors of the following, in which these poems appear.

South Florida Poetry Journal: "Dear Sociopath"

African American Review: "Angela Davis Was in My Car" and "Zora Neale Hurston"

Cutbank Literary Journal: "Talisman" and "Open Your Mouth"

The print anthology *Goodbye:* "Rebuilding Mother"

Literary Mama: "My Mother's Advice"

Meridians: feminism, race, transnationalism: "Open Your Mouth"

Rogue Agent: "Inheritance"

Scapegoat Review: "Sweet and Low"

South Florida Poetry Journal: "Eagle Ray"

Superstition Review: "To Watch Her Face Fall"

Torch Literary Arts: "Black Person Head Bob"

The Pushcart Prize XLIX: Best of the Small Presses (Wainscott, NY: Pushcart Press, 2024): "Black Person Head Bob"

Typehouse: "My Mother and I Save Our Yogurt Containers to Reuse Them," "Brown Girl," "We Are Very Witchy," and "To Watch the Till Movie"

Viewless Wings: "Hammerhead"

"For You" and "The Necromancer Returns in Distress" were first published in *Alien(s)*, as a Bottlecap Feature, Bottlecap Press 2023.

A special thank-you to *Torch Literary Arts* and *The Pushcart Prize* for recognizing my poem, "Black Person Head Bob." It was easily my most rejected poem. I am so grateful to them for seeing value in this work and for the opportunity to amplify this important poem.

Abundant gratitude to my mentors, Julie Marie Wade, Lynne Barrett, Richard Blanco, Denise Duhamel, and Les Standiford. Without them, I would not be a poet.

Special thanks to Lisa Williams, who saw promise in my unwieldy manuscript. And thank-you to Patrick O'Dowd for patiently helping me to bring this book into the world.

Thank-you to my son Jordan for being himself and my star.